# *How To Raise Your Child Like A Jamaican*

(Life lessons my parents taught me)

## Dahlia D. Welsh

Edited by Dawn Comer Jefferson and Rosanne Welch

Photography by Yoshi Makino

Cover and Interior Artwork by Yuka Izutsu

Copyright © 2005 by Dahlia D. Welsh

Artwork copyright © 2007 by Dahlia D. Welsh

Published by Dahlia D. Welsh

Library of Congress Cataloging-in-Publication Data available.

ISBN: 978-0-6151-4761-1


First printing, 2007

Printed in the U.S.A.

*Me, Alecia and Sophia*

*Locksley and Ilene Welsh*

*Stafford and Lucy Samuels*

*Louise and Charles Welsh*

# FOREWORD
## *By Devon Harris*
### (Three-Time Olympian, Author, Motivational Speaker)

When Dahlia asked me to provide a foreword to this book, it came as a pleasant surprise. Nonetheless, I was deeply honored and was more than happy to do so. You are about to embark on an experience that, as the title of this book suggests, highlights the subtle and not so subtle nuances of child rearing Jamaican style. As I read through the pages, I was transported back to many aspects of my own childhood, and I smiled many times at the similarities in the upbringing of a child in Jamaica and a child being raised by Jamaican parents in the middle of Brooklyn, New York. As a parent, I was also struck by how those valuable lessons I learnt growing up have influenced my interactions with my own children.

All children come to us without instructions. That makes parenting and child rearing one of the most daunting, complicated undertakings of all. Given the complex demands of society, defining good parenting skills with hard and fast rules is, at best, difficult because there is often a wide disparity between cultures. Likewise, parenting skills differ from one person to the next, and dealing with each child presents its own unique set of challenges as well.

Love, self-discipline, nourishment, a secure home, a sense of community, and personal pride are only some of the things parents give to their children as they prepare the next generation to run the planet.

In this book, Dahlia provides some insight into how Jamaicans tackle the ominous duty of parenting. Her personal stories and anecdotes will not only amuse and entertain; they will also inform and educate.

Sit back, relax and enjoy!

# BIG UPS

As we say in Jamaica, I would like to *big up* my grandparents Lucy Olivier 'Miss Ella' Samuels, Stafford 'Doctor' Samuels, Louise 'Sister Lou' Welsh and Charles 'Busha' Welsh. I want to big up my parents, Ilene and Locksley Welsh for leading by example. To my sisters, Sophia and Alecia, big ups for always watching over me, keeping me out of harm's way and making our childhood fun.

And last, but not least, much love and 'nuff respect to mothers, fathers and all others serving in the role of parent. Raising a child is not easy, but hopefully this book will present a new perspective on the world's first 'oldest profession' - parenting.

# TABLE OF CONTENTS

# IRIE!

One night, my dad and I were talking about a reality TV show where a young woman had to take off her clothes for the chance to win $50,000, not a guarantee of getting the money, just a shot. My dad was offended by her lack of judgment, so I assured him that he would never have to worry about any of his daughters taking off their clothes for money. My dad's response was, "I know none of you would do that, because the next time I saw you I would bust you in your lip." For your information, most of our conversations include thinly veiled threats told in jest... sort of.

We soon got on to the topic of why my sisters and I would never act like the young woman on the TV show and that conversation became the inspiration for this book. I told my dad that he and my mother were so tough on us that our household was run like a military academy. My dad laughed and said that they may have been tough, but we turned out pretty good. I half-heartedly laughed and replied that he was right, but there were times when I didn't think I would make it through the 'Welsh Academy of Child Rearing.'

And so if my upbringing was like going through a military academy, what would be the lessons I learned? How have those lessons influenced my life? How might they influence yours? With these questions in mind, I've put together these tips and quips from the W.A.C.R. I don't have a degree in child rearing and 'Me no have chick nor child,' but what I do have is the knowledge and wisdom of my parents, grandparents, aunts and uncles who through their actions and words taught me these informative and funny Jamaican life lessons.

## **<u>Chapter One</u>**

# If You Know Your History, Then You Would Know Where You're Coming From

# "WE ARE JAMAICANS, WHO ARE YOU?"

Let's face it, siblings can be mean. My sisters used to taunt me by singing, "We are Jamaicans who are you?" I was the youngest and although we lived in America, I was the only Yankee in the family. They used to sing about the beautiful waters of Jamaica, cool breezes and mango trees. The best I could do in retaliation was threaten to call INS, but for the record, my family has always been in this country legally. Do you know your family tree? Do you know the town in Ireland where your grandfather was born? Your mom is part Croatian, but can you find it on a map? According to family records, I am from the Ashanti of Ghana and a descendant of the Maroons of Jamaica. How many people know where they're from?

A lot of people liken America to a melting pot, while others say it is more like a tossed salad. I personally prefer the latter analogy because it allows for individuality. It leaves room for people's histories. Teach your child about their family history. Knowing where they come from will help to build pride and a strong sense of who they are. Not only should children know their history, they should be able to touch the soil, walk the streets and breathe the air of those who came before them.

Every time I go to Jamaica, I feel such a strong connection to the island and the people even though I wasn't born there. I walk through the house where my mother grew up and if I close my eyes; I can see her as a child sitting on the veranda looking out at the Santa Cruz Mountains. The best gifts that my parents gave me are their stories of what it was like growing up in Jamaica. Hearing their stories solidifies my connection to a land and a people who help define me.

I used to wonder where I got off sticking up for myself when others allowed themselves to be used as doormats. I wasn't always this confident, but it was like something kicked into high gear during my late twenties. Then it struck me that it was the Maroon in me coming out. On my father's side of the family I am a Maroon. Maroon is a term used to refer to runaway slaves, mostly in the Caribbean, who rebelled against their oppressors.

In Jamaica, they escaped into the mountains, fought off invasions by the Spanish and English and were able to set up their own societies. There were some limitations regarding how they were able to govern themselves and the conditions for their existence were outlined in a treaty. About two years ago, my family and I went to Accompong which is the largest Jamaican Maroon town located in St. Elizabeth – my mother's hometown. We were able to walk the grounds of our ancestors, see the places where they hid and fought off attacks from invaders and see how the town still thrives.

There are five Maroon towns in Jamaica and to this day, they operate much like they did in the past. The Accompong tour was exciting; I purchased a copy of the original treaty that was drawn up between the Maroons and the British. It is framed and hanging on the wall of my sanctuary at home. Learning about my history firsthand, solidified for me who I am and where I'm coming from.

# ODE TO MS. ELLA BAILEY

I was in Jamaica a couple of years ago, and we were at the hospital for my grandfather's yearly physical – my grandmother had already passed away. While waiting, I struck up a conversation with an older gentleman, Mr. Parks. As we continued to chat, I told him that I was Ms. Ella's granddaughter. A smile spread across his face because he knew my grandmother from the years she used to work at the hospital. As it turns out, my grandmother cared for Mr. Parks during his frequent visits. Mr. Parks told me that sometimes at night; the only thing that would help him sleep was a glass of warm water. According to him, no matter what my grandmother was doing, she always brought him water. He went on to say how wonderful and caring she was.

With that said, I can't begin to explain how honored I felt to hear a total stranger speak so highly of my grandmother. He made her out to be an angel, which she was and even in death she continues to make me proud to call myself Ms. Ella's granddaughter. It is important that children know that they don't live in a vacuum and that the good or bad that they do, has an effect on them and can affect those around them. They should act with respect for themselves, in all situations. If we think about the impression we will leave behind, we can walk through the world consciously. How will your child be remembered? If they always put their best foot forward, then you won't have to worry.

# GRANNY NANNY

Most people outside of Jamaica don't know who Granny Nanny is, but she was declared a Jamaican national hero in 1975. Granny Nanny, or Queen Nanny, along with her five brothers was a revolt leader during the maroon wars that took place during the 1700s. Through the use of guerilla warfare, she helped free many slaves and assisted in defeating the British, in battle after battle. She is a great role model for anyone needing inspiration.

My role models growing up and even to this day are so close to home, they either have the same last name as me or have my mother's maiden name. My dad loves photography, he used to have a Nikon camera and we would go out to Prospect Park and take pictures all day long. I remember him wanting to convert a closet into a dark room, but my mom wasn't about to give up any of her precious shoe space. Seeing my dad showing his creative side and being passionate about something, encouraged me to find my passion.

As I child, I soaked up everything around me including what my parents said and did. Their values are my values, their morals are my morals. Children need role models that are close to home. Although raised in the U.S., I have not strayed far from my parents' traditional Jamaican ways. In short, my parents were and are, the shining example of the person they want me to be.

# ACKEE AND SALT FISH

One of the great things about living in the U.S. is that you don't have to leave the country or in some cases your own neighborhood to experience different cultures. Growing up in Brooklyn, I had friends from Puerto Rico, Dominican Republic, China, Korea, Panama, Haiti, Russia and even Albania! When I was young, my best friend was from Puerto Rico and I remember her joining us for a dinner of oxtails, rice and peas. I also remember going to her house one day for dinner and sitting down to arroz con pollo - chicken with rice. But this rice was orange. I had never seen orange rice before so I decided not to eat it. Everyone was eating and talking and no one died from eating it, so I tasted a forkful. It was delicious. To this day, I remember being so fascinated by the orange rice that I ran home and when my mom asked me how dinner was; all I could talk about was the orange rice. I later learned that the rice turned orange because of the tomatoes used when it was prepared.

My parents encouraged our understanding of other cultures by welcoming our friends into our home. They took us to festivals and to see movies by artists from different countries. Expose your children to as many different cultures as possible. By doing so, hopefully you will minimize prejudices because it's hard to hate a person after you've broken bread with them.

# BANANAFANAFEFIFOFANA

I was at a holiday party when a pregnant woman approached me because she heard that my family was Jamaican. She was excited because she and her husband were having a hard time coming up with names for their child and they loved the way Jamaican names were often very proper. I gave her some ideas for naming her child like a Jamaican: Winston (every Jamaican family has one), Wadsworth, Sean, Lance (short for Lancelot), Barrington, Sharon, Locksley, Marcia, Nadine and Oliver. There is no mistaking how to spell these names and isn't school hard enough without adding to it a name that is not only phonetically incorrect, but just flat out spelled wrong? There is no guarantee that if your child's name is jacked up, yes I said jacked up, they won't succeed, but why take the chance?

I worked with a woman who wanted to name her daughter S'sense and then got upset when I couldn't figure out that S'sense should be pronounced Essence. I had another co-worker that was so into the soap opera 'The Young and the Restless' that she named her son Blade, after one of the characters.

So please, stop the madness before we end up with a child named Bananafanafeefifofanabanana. You may say what about Condoleeza, Oprah and Barack? Well, these names are definitely off the beaten path, but if you notice none of them reference a weapon and all of them are spelled phonetically correct. A name says a lot about a person. Did you know that Barack means blessed, in Swahili?

# IT TAKES A WHOLE VILLAGE
# TO RAISE A CHILD

*- African Proverb*

Whenever I go to Jamaica I feel the close ties it has with its African roots. From the food I eat, to some of the words that are a part of Jamaican patois. So it makes 'It takes a whole village to raise a child' really ring true. I remember being too young to go home directly after school, so my parents came up with an alternative. My sisters and I would go to the library, until they picked us up. The library on Linden Boulevard, off of Church Avenue in Brooklyn was where we would go to do our homework. We were also able to take part in the R.I.F., Reading Is Fundamental, program that encouraged young readers.

There was an added perk of going to the library – we became friends with someone who turned into one of the most influential people in our lives, Ms. Smith, the librarian. She would help us with our homework and when it was time for her to go home at five o'clock; we would sometimes walk with her to the train station, which was right next to our apartment building. I remember Ms. Smith waiting until we were safely inside our building before heading home.

One of my fondest memories of Ms. Smith was when she gave us a book with no words entitled, 'Pancakes for Breakfast'. It was great because we made up our own words to go along with the pictures, which encouraged our young imaginations. A friend of Ms. Smith's wrote the book, so she was able to get him to autograph it, which to us was a big deal.

No one asked Ms. Smith to take on any extra duties and our relationship with her existed with my parents' approval. We were very well behaved; so whether Ms. Smith was at the library or not, we would never have acted badly because back in those days news traveled quickly through the village. However, as it turns out, Ms. Smith, who started off as a stranger, actually became a perfect example of a village elder helping to raise a couple of the children in the village.

## **Chapter Two**

I've Been Working Since My
Eyes Were Down At My Knees!

# EVERY MIKKLE MAKES A MUCKLE

*(A Penny Saved Is A Penny Earned)*

My five-year-old nephew came to visit from Georgia. He had saved about $40 so he'd have some pocket money. While at a department store, he saw a toy he wanted and I reminded him that he had money in his wallet, but he said all I had to do is pay for it by sliding my (credit) card. He has a savings account at the bank, knows how to deposit checks and with the help of my sister, did put money aside for the trip. However, he still needed to be reminded, 'Every mikkle makes a muckle'. Teach your children early about the principles of money. They may not grasp the concept by age five, but at least they'll be on the right path. Make sure that they know that ATMs and credit cards don't give away free money.

I used to get an allowance and it was an effective way to teach me the value of money. My parents made the amount I was given equal to my needs and not my wants, i.e. I needed lunch money for school and wanted Sassoon jeans. I was also expected to save some of the money.

If I burned through my money before the next 'pay period,' my parents didn't go easy on me - remember they're Jamaican. In real life, what happens when you don't have the money to cover your expenses? You either go into debt or go without. To this day, my dad doesn't have a credit card and if my mother has to take a dollar out of her savings account; you better believe that she's the first person she pays back the next time she receives her pay check. It's best that children learn money management skills when they're young, rather than when they're sixty with less than a decade to retire.

# 'YARD' CLOTHES

With two older sisters, clothes that started off as pants on my sister Sophia turned into high waters by the time they reached my sister Alecia and became capris by the time they came to me. Hand me downs weren't that bad sometimes, because there was the added bonus of having an ever expanding wardrobe. And my mother, being the over explainer that she is, told my sisters and I that because we're all girls, it was okay for us to wear the same shirts, pants, skirts, bra and shoes. However, we were never to share the same underwear. Even to this day, I can't get over that last part because I think that was pretty obvious.

In my family nothing went to waste, so hand me down clothing was a part of life. If the clothes were too faded, too tight or too short to be worn to school or church they became our 'yard' clothes, - clothes that we wore around the house or maybe outside to play. Nowadays, wearing secondhand clothes is considered chic. I guess back then we were ahead of the times.

# REJECTS THEY COST
# A DOLLAR NINETY-NINE

While everyone else was wearing Sergio Valente, Jordache and Cross Colors (yes, I am that old) I went to school in mostly no name clothing. Have you heard of Rejects? They were plain white sneakers with no pizzazz whatsoever. Rejects were so popular among the low income set that they had their own song, *"Rejects they cost a dollar ninety-nine, Rejects they make your feet feel fine."*

When it came to name brand clothes, my parents never entertained the idea of buying us the hip and trendy stuff. My mom and dad would always say that they were not going to pay big money so that we could walk around with someone else's name on our backsides. My mom was fond of saying, "Those who want Jordache jeans should go out and get a job, so that they can make the money to pay for Jordache jeans." So that meant looking fly was basically out of the question. If you buy your children clothing mainly for special occasions, i.e. birthday and Christmas and not indulge every expensive whim they have, hopefully it will begin to teach them to not determine their worth based on their wardrobe.

# EVERY JAMAICAN HAS AT LEAST TWO

When I was growing up in New York City you could get your working papers at the age of fourteen. That means that as of this writing, I have been paying into the system for twenty-one years. When I hit my second decade of servitude, I made a point of 'thanking' my parents for making me get a job at such an early age.

My first job was with the Police Athletic League's summer camp. I had previously attended the program as a camper so I already had a certain level of comfort. And truth be told, it was actually pretty fun because it got me out of the house during the hot humid summer months and I made money, albeit very little after taxes, but it was still something. What was the starting wage in New York City back in 1984? A whopping $3.35! And then of course, my mom swooped in to jack us for money to save for back to school clothes, etc.

To teach children the value of a dollar take one child, mix in a job as soon as they're old enough to legally work, then stir in the shock and disbelief they will have once they get their first paycheck. Once children realize that Uncle Sam has eaten up the money from all those hours of hard work, hopefully they'll come to appreciate an honest day's work for an honest day's pay.

If you mention to some parents that their children should work, they clutch their pearls like you're asking to burn them at the stake, but let's be honest, you wouldn't teach your child how to swim by describing to them what to do on dry land, right? So how can you effectively teach them the value of a dollar if they aren't the ones earning it? Besides, a couple of days having to abide by someone else's rules in order to get some financial freedom will help put life in perspective.

The decision to work was not left up to me and cannot be left up to your child because working actually requires work and accountability, two things you normally don't associate with children. Working at the age of fourteen gave me a jump on life because it helped me to develop a strong work ethic, i.e. showing up on time and being accountable.

# HOW MUCH ARE TREE TREES?

At random times and I mean completely random times during the day, my mom would test me and my sisters on our times tables to see if we could multiply quickly in our heads. There are several things that go along with being a savvy consumer and knowing math is one of them. If sugar was on sale for a dollar a pound with a two-bag limit, my mother would give me and my sisters money and have us go through the grocery line separately. I was always afraid that we were doing something illegal but we weren't, we were just being savvy consumers by buying when prices were low.

We didn't have a whole lot of money, so when summer came and we needed new clothes, my mom would give us $20 each, yes $20, and send us out shopping for shorts and tees. Now back in those days, $20 could go a long way if you were savvy and shopped at Bobby's Department Store on Church Avenue. We would calculate our item prices carefully and take tax into account because $20 was all we had. My budget has gotten bigger, but my practice is still the same. I set aside a certain amount of money each week for groceries, with not too wide a margin for error. As I put items in my cart I round up and do the math in my head and 95% of the time I am within my budget.

For the record, tree trees equal nine.

## YOU HAVE FI RISE
## WHEN COCK A CROW

When I was a child, we used to spend summers in Jamaica. Now you might think how great, sandy beaches and all the mangoes you can eat, no problem, Mon! Well, not so quick. My summers in Jamaica consisted of waking up when 'the cock a crow' which meant when the sun was rising; and because my grandparents didn't have electricity we had to utilize as much daylight as possible. We got up, ate breakfast, usually cornmeal porridge or fish and some hard dough bread and then we had to take the cows to pasture. After that we went out to the fields to pick peanuts. Pick peanuts? I'm from Brooklyn, what did I know about picking peanuts? I could pick a jar of peanuts off the shelf at the supermarket. I could also buy and open the jar, but pick them? It was hard, backbreaking work, not to mention we were out in the hot sun. But that's how you cultivate work ethic in a child, by putting them to work.

My parents also instilled good habits in us that played along with the life lessons. They made sure that we woke up early, even on the weekends. We had to wake up and clean the house and only after our chores were done could we watch 'The Super Friends', 'Captain Caveman and the Teen Angels' or go outside to play.

# A GOOD ROUTINE GOES A LONG WAY

As a child, everyday, when my mother got home from school she had a set routine. She had two choices. The first was to take a penny and walk up to the church with a bucket, where she bought water and carried it back home on her head. I've made that journey to the church without a bucket on my head and trust me, the church is not up the block – it's a serious hike. The second choice was to load up the donkey with two hampers - plastic buckets - ride it to town where she would buy water and carry it back to the house. My dad's situation was pretty much the same. He had to take a bucket to a standing pipe and carry water back to his house. After hearing their stories my first reaction was, "Boy you sure were some water in a bucket, carrying people." My second reaction was to feel silly that I once complained about having to hang up my clothes and do homework after school.

My sisters and I didn't have to carry heavy buckets of water back and forth but we did have routines that became second nature. Nowadays, just like when I was growing up, when I get home from work I leave my shoes at the door, change out of my work clothes into something more comfortable – 'yard clothes', pack my lunch and pick out my clothes for work the next day. Having set routines like the ones my parents taught, me take some of the guesswork out of everyday life and are helpful no matter what age you are.

# YOU NUH FI TEK DIS FOR A JOKE

*(Serious matters, i.e. giving and receiving)*

My nephew had a fundraiser at school. He sent a thank you card for every person who bought an item. The lesson that was instilled was to be appreciative of gifts and gestures from others. My parents had a house rule, we couldn't play with a toy, spend money or wear an item of clothing until my sisters and I called the gift giver to say thank you. This is common courtesy and anything less than a thank you seems ungrateful. I always have a box of small note cards handy, just in case I need to say thank you for the gift, or thank you for taking the time to meet with me, or thank you for welcoming me into your home.

Another important lesson I learned about giving happened years ago; when my dad sent me a hundred dollars because I was going through a rough patch. Trying to be considerate, I tore up the check because I knew he could probably use the hundred dollars, too. I felt good about my actions until a friend explained that my father sending me the check was not about the money, but about him as my father wanting to give his daughter something she needed. By tearing up the check, I didn't provide him with the opportunity to give. When you don't allow yourself to receive from others, whether its money, a favor or love, you're not allowing them to give. And no matter what the culture, it's always better to give than to receive.

## **<u>Chapter Three</u>**

# Mi Come Fi Drink Milk,
# Mi No Come Fi Count Cow
*(Be straightforward in your interactions)*

# YOU ALWAYS DID TINK
# YOUR POOP FI MAKE PATTYS
*(Don't co-sign their b.s.)*

My parents used to tell us that if we got into serious trouble and were hauled off to jail, not to call them because they were not going to bail us out. To this day, I don't know if they were serious, but none of us ever put their threat to the test.

Parents can be the biggest enablers on the planet because they never want to believe that their children can do any wrong. I have a cousin who got into serious trouble and for the longest time, my aunt would blame her friends. Deep down, she knew her daughter was up to no good, but refused to believe it until it was too late to help. When your child does something wrong, don't let them off easy and 'Don't cosign their B.S.' When you stop your child from facing the music and constantly rush in to save the day, then you are cosigning their bad behavior. It makes me cringe when I see parents defend a child who they know has done wrong. Let 'em hang - not literally of course - but let them know that mom and dad are not going to use their power and influence to get them out of trouble every time.

When a situation didn't sit right with my father, he would say, "You mean to tell me…" and then re-iterate my version of events. I would have to repeat my story and he would mull it over, again and again; like an interrogator seeing if the facts changed. If after the water torture treatment he still didn't hear what he liked, he'd move onto electroshock therapy – just kidding, sort of. But the truth of the matter was that if what you said didn't make sense, he wasn't going to be taken for a fool. My dad had no problem calling friends, their parents and teachers to fact check my story.

If your child's story doesn't pass the smell test, then become a detective. Check out every inch of their story. If they come home late and say it's because Suzie's car broke down, question every one separately to get to the bottom of the story. This is your chance to play detective. Remember, no one respects a pushover. If your children know that you are going to go the extra mile to get to the truth and that you will mete out consequences, they won't be as inclined to break your rules.

# A BAG OF MOUTH

When we were younger and when we promised our parents that we were going to do something, we were held to our word. We weren't allowed to just be a 'bag of mouth' spewing promises we had no intention of keeping. Point out when their words don't match their actions. Our perception of ourselves usually differs from who we really are. As a parent, it's your job to help your children see the truth about who they are. If they say they are going to work hard at school, point out when they've spent more time hanging out with friends and chatting on the phone than studying.

When my sister Sophia was in junior high school, she had an opportunity to be in an accelerated class. Although she said she wanted to be part of the faster track, her grades didn't reflect that. My mom finally called her bluff and told her teachers that since hanging out with her friends was more important than working hard, they should keep her on the regular track.

At the end of the day, if we don't have clothes on our back or even food to eat, sometimes our word is all we have. Be true to your word and when it comes to your children; don't make excuses when they don't follow through on theirs. Instead, let them bear the consequences.

# HIM NUH FI COME AND WAIT

On a recent trip to Jamaica; my maternal grandfather, uncle and I were making plans to visit my sister in Kingston. My uncle promised to pick us up at eight am the next morning. As soon as the time was set, grandpa said, "We can't let him come and wait. We have to be on time." Little did I know that phrase would be constantly repeated. That night, grandpa kept vigil on the time by clicking his flashlight off and on, even though the alarm was set. Grandpa got up at six a.m., said his prayers and then announced, "Don't let Uncle come and wait," and with that, he was off to the bathroom to get ready.

My parents also did not play when it came to bedtime. We had to have our homework done, clothes picked out for the next day and be ready for bed by eight p.m. sharp - there was little variation from the schedule. My sisters and I wanted to watch TV, but that wasn't allowed during the weekday because my parents did not tolerate sleepy children. As a matter of fact, it worked in our best interest to wake up before the alarm, because I truly believe that my mom got a secret pleasure out of turning on the lights, ripping back the covers and yelling, "Get up now!" As a rule, I'm usually early or exactly on time and I have little patience for lateness because it seems to be so disrespectful of other people's time.

# WANTI WANTI CAN'T GET IT, GETTI GETTI NO WANT IT

*(The haves and the have-nots)*

My parents made it very clear that we weren't going to get everything our little hearts desired. And they really played their hand when Christmas came around. I would tell them what I wanted and they would question if I had been naughty or nice enough to even deserve presents. Let me tell you, I spent some serious time in my youth reflecting about the error of my ways.

My parents never tried to buy our affection. Recently, a friend who has had trouble holding down a job bought her underage, learner's permit son, a car. She was so proud of herself. All kinds of thoughts flooded into my brain, like why? Why? And why? She wanted to buy his affection. Why else would she make an unsafe and unwise decision that could potentially jeopardize the financial health of an entire family? My parents, whether consciously or unconsciously made the decision early on whether they wanted to be cool and 'down' parents or teaching, molding, disciplinarian parents - they chose the latter. Don't let the first time your child hears the word 'no' be from a stranger. Life is full of road blocks; let them learn how to deal with them from you.

## **<u>Chapter Four</u>**

# Time Longer Than Rope

*(You must crawl before you can walk)*

# THREE MEALS A DAY NO WIFE TO OBEY
*(Being independent)*

From the time I came out of the womb, I knew I only had eighteen years to live at home, before I had to strike out on my own. How do you raise independent children? Do as my parents did, raise them in stages. When they are young, treat them as children. When they are adolescents, treat them as young adults and at the age of eighteen, show them the door! One of the biggest disservices you can do to your child, is to not prepare them for a life without you around 24/7.

Eighteen years is long enough to come up with a strong idea of what direction they would like their life to take. Tell your children often and be firm that when they turn eighteen, they will be adults so they should be prepared to leave home. As my parents put it, we had tree (three) choices: college, the military or the door, because we were not going to live at home and work. If we wanted to work, we had to leave home and make our own way. Before the time came for us to stand on our own two feet, our parents made our lives so unbearable we couldn't wait to move out.

Continue to treat your children as children; curfews and all. Don't pamper them by doing laundry, cooking, cleaning and running errands for them and if they are going to live at home, they should be required to have a job and contribute towards rent and utilities.

I left home at seventeen to go to college and that was important because it was my first taste of independence. Fast-forward eight years later and there I was in the heart of the country's capital ready to sign the lease to my first apartment. It was one of the scariest moments in my life. Up until that time, I had never lived alone. Growing up, I shared a room with my sisters and in college I always had roommates, but now here I was by myself. From here on out, I would be completely responsible for the bills, the trash, the dishes, everything.

Responsibility and self-doubt can be very daunting, even if you are well prepared. I faltered and reconsidered my decision to not have a roommate, but in the end I stood on my own two feet. I was twenty-five, living in D.C. and I knew that deep down, this was something I was groomed for and always wanted. I ended up not only rising to the challenge, but I absolutely loved living by myself. And being able to live by yourself often comes with the added bonus of a 'get out of jail free' card. A 'pass' that allows me to walk away from any crappy living situation because I know I can live on my own.

# GONE A FOREIGN

The first time I traveled without my parents, I was five years old. My sisters and I went to Jamaica to visit family. They put us on Air Jamaica with strict instructions to not speak to anyone. They introduced us to the flight attendants and off we went. So now I have no problem packing a bag and heading off to any destination, be it the library or that wonderful four-day solo trip to Maui I took on my twenty-eighth birthday.

My sister is starting to nurture the independent side of my three-year-old nephew. Recently, she sent him from Georgia to Brooklyn on a surprise visit to my mom's house. He went with his best friend and an older family friend who used to baby-sit him. My sister was there with him at the airport, but obviously neither she nor my brother-in-law were on the plane. Now keep in mind, my nephew had already traveled to Florida, Jamaica and New York so he was no stranger to waking up in a new locale, but he is still a child.

For several weeks leading up to the trip, my sister kept telling my nephew that when he got on the plane, mommy won't be there and daddy won't be there and when he got to New York, mommy won't be there and daddy won't be there, only Nana. So by the time the trip came around, he was ready and actually looking forward to helping Nana shovel snow. He was only in New York for a long weekend, but there were absolutely no problems.

After his trip to visit my mom, I asked him if he would visit me in California. I told him it would be like when he visited Nana, that mommy won't be here and daddy won't be here and he was fine. Especially after I threw in a trip to Disneyland and a dinner of shrimp and crabs – the boy has expensive taste - but all the same I got a resounding yes, from a three-year-old!

Whether you send your child to visit family in another country or in another state, it is a great confidence builder to give them the opportunity to travel and spend time away from you and their comfort zone. Being out of arm's reach will help them grow into strong, independent people.

## WHY YOU WANT PUT ME IN A QUART WHEN PINT CAN HOLD ME?

I was sitting at home one night, several years ago. It was a Saturday night and I was bored out of my skull and my friend had just cancelled our movie date. As I settled in to another night of TV, I realized that my legs weren't broken. I had money in my pocket so there was no reason why I should sit at home when I could go to the movie.

When I arrived at the theatre and asked for one ticket I was self-conscious at first, but then I soon realized that no one was paying attention to me. It was opening night and the usual seat saving was going on in the packed theatre, but that didn't apply to me because I needed only one seat in the center, mid-way from the screen. It was perfect.

What I realized that night was that my parents had groomed me my whole life to strike out and be independent. The first 'test' was when I went away to college. They were absolutely right when they would say, "Why allow yourself to be put in a quart, when a pint can hold you?" Whether it's self imposed or something they allow others to do to them, if you can instill in your child the value of living without bounds, you will open up a new world to them, a world that's theirs for the taking.

## **<u>Chapter Five</u>**

You Go To School To Learn,
Not Put On a Fashion Show

# ME THROW ME CORN
# BUT ME NO CALL NO FOWL
*(Actions speak louder than words)*

People will sleep outside to get tickets to a concert. Lines will snake around blocks for the next installment of the latest hit movie. Everyone says they want what's best for their children, but how many people put their money where their mouths are?

I can't remember where my zoned high school was, but I know that Mahalia Jackson Junior High School, on East New York Avenue in Brooklyn was better. So, by hook or by crook my parents, okay my mother, did what she had to do to make sure I received the best education. Mahalia Jackson had great teachers and they had a program that would allow me to do something I always wanted to do, which was skip a grade. At Mahalia Jackson Junior High, a.k.a. P.S. 391, you could skip a grade by essentially doing three academic years in the time span of two. I did all the work of a seventh grader and half that of an eighth grader in the seventh grade. Then I did the other half of the eighth grade and all of the ninth in the ninth grade, thereby doing three years in two.

It was intense, but because my parents had instilled the value of education since day one, I was up for the challenge. That foundation of my parents' support and the quality education I received prepared me for my next step, which was attending one of the top high schools in New York City, Brooklyn Technical. My parents didn't just say that education was of the utmost importance, they actively sought out better schools and by doing that they showed me that actions speak louder than words.

# ELECTRICITY NUH GROW PON TREES!

"If you tink you're going to sit in this house using up all my electricity, you have another tink coming!" Question? Can you really use up all the electricity? My mom used to act like my sisters and I had some sort of conspiracy to run up the electric bill. She would yell at us for leaving a room and not turning off the light and she would always find an activity that didn't require using light. Like reading, that could be done by the window and playing outside and better yet, go to the library and use up their electricity!

If you think your school age children can't behave for long periods of time without the latest PlayStation, think again. When I was growing up, we didn't have Atari. The only time I played video games was at a friend's home or when I went with my mom to the bowling alley. Reading was my parents' cure for childhood boredom and I have carried that lesson with me throughout my life. To this day, I take a book or magazine with me whenever I know I might be subjected to waiting, like at the D.M.V. The result of all that reading was evident because in school I always tested above my grade level in reading and vocabulary. My sisters and I were so hooked on reading that we fought to determine who would read the Sunday comics and the 'Ebony' and 'Jet' magazines first.

A love for reading should be started early and encouraged at every step. My parents didn't just tell us to read, every night my dad would read the newspaper and my mom was hooked on romance novels. A couple of years ago, while talking to my sister Sophia, I asked about the whereabouts of my nephew. Sophia replied that he was in his room reading. Reading? He was only two at the time.

I am sure that most aunts think their nephews are geniuses, but reading at the age of two? He hadn't even mastered potty training! So I asked her, "Can he read?" her response was, "No, but he doesn't know it. He's 'reading' a book that makes noise when he chooses the correct colors and shapes." Two years later, as he approached his fourth year, I asked my nephew what he wanted for his birthday. His answer, "A Spider Man book." What is the message? Start them young and they will develop an affinity for almost anything. The same may not hold true for broccoli.

# NINCOMPOOP!
# AND OTHER DIRTY WORDS

One day while reading the newspaper, my dad, sister Alecia and I got into a discussion, I can't remember the topic, but I do remember an exasperated Alecia saying to my dad, "Don't be such a nincompoop!" One of the many rules in our home was that you could not use a word that was not in the dictionary. That ruled out words like, "Huh?" and "Wha?" We were also not supposed to use words if we didn't know their meaning.

My father asked Alecia if she knew what a nincompoop was and when she shook her head, he told her to look it up in the dictionary. Being a little busybody and not one to miss any action, I followed Alecia to the bookshelf. We already had an idea of what it meant, but I guess Alecia was hoping for a miracle. With baited breath, Alecia looked up nincompoop in the dictionary. Upon reading the meaning, her face dropped as if she had seen a ghost. Right there in bold print, nincompoop was defined as a fool. I patted her on the back with sympathy because I knew she was finished.

As my father waited for her to define nincompoop, Alecia slowly walked back to him like she was on a death march. My father put the newspaper aside, "Well, what does it mean?" With all the strength she could muster, Alecia replied, "It's… it's not in the dictionary." I must've been in a good mood because I didn't rat her out. As I recounted this story to my dad many years later; he revealed that he knew what the word meant, but that he decided to cut her a break. My parents were tough on us most of the time, but I guess part of the deal is knowing when to 'tek it easy.' To this day, when I bring up this story for a good laugh, oddly enough Alecia doesn't find it funny.

# MEK SURE YOUR DRAWERS DEM NUH DUTTY

In our little two-bedroom apartment on Caton Avenue, my parents were able to somehow recreate Jamaican living. We had a washer but no dryer, so after clothes were washed we had to string up a clothesline that ran from the front door to my parents' bedroom. While one of us carried the clothes, one person pinned them to the clothesline and the other went back and forth to the washing machine getting more clothes.

Teaching your child how to do laundry is the gift that keeps on giving. Not only will it alleviate some of the load on you, it will teach them to take care of their clothing. If they ruin a shirt or a pair of pants in the wash, they'll miss it big time when they go to their closet to wear it. The more skills children are sent out into the world with the less you have to worry if they're doing all right. Besides, my mom didn't believe in doing everything around the house, especially with three daughters who could help.

# YOUR HEAD FAVOR ROOSTER PICKNEY

When I was fifteen, my parents separated. My older sisters were away at college, so I was left to deal with my father physically leaving our home, all by myself. I was very sad, withdrawn and acted out by wearing a Mohawk - yes, black people sport Mohawks, too - what can I say, it was the '80's. Do allow your children to express themselves through their clothes and style. However, limit self-expression to temporary things that they won't have to live with for the rest of their lives i.e., crazy tattoos on their hands and face, excessive piercings and ear stretching. These forms of self-expression are not acceptable for children because they may hinder their ability to support themselves later in life. Besides, what looks cool at sixteen isn't so cool all stretched out and disfigured at seventy-five.

Altering my appearance didn't lead to drug use or hanging out with the wrong crowd because the ground rules had already been set. My Mohawk helped me grieve the passing of my parents' relationship. Children change their appearances for many different reasons - a need to fit in, isolation, a bad home life, parents' divorcing - how you react to it can make the stage a passing fad or a statement of resentment. Talk to your children, let them know you care, let them cry on your shoulder. Eventually, I stopped mourning my parents' break up because I realized that the end of their marriage did not signal the end of my relationship with my father.

# BATTY A HANG OUT A DOOR

When I was growing up, Madonna, The Mary Jane Girls and Vanity 6 were the hot girl groups.  In high school, I was invited to a friend's sixteenth birthday party.  As a special treat, my mother bought me my first pair of Italian shoes - black patent leather Bandalinos.  All I needed was the dress, so I scoured my Right On! and Tiger Beat magazines for something to wear and found a dress that Vanity from Vanity 6 was wearing.  It had spaghetti straps and was all lace with a see through skirt.  You couldn't see the family jewels but you could see her legs almost to the top.

I showed the dress to my mother and she approved so we went to get it made.  My mother explained to the dressmaker what we needed and added, "We'll need some material to line the bottom of the dress." My face must've dropped when I realized I was not going to walk around with my goodies exposed like one of Prince's protégés because my mother gave me a look that said, "I know you don't tink you're going fi walk around with your batty a hang out a door like de woman inna dis magazine?"  I smiled and agreed that the dress needed more coverage.

Make sure that your children's clothes are age appropriate.  When your daughter sits down in a skirt if her bare backside hits the seat or your son's pants are so low you can see his underwear, then you should probably help them re-evaluate their choice of attire.

## Chapter Six

# We Rule Tings,
# Tings Nuh Rule We!

# EVERYTHING FROM THE HEAD COOK TO THE BOTTLE WASHER

Having both parents from the same island is like having two parents that were raised in the same household. My parents may have disagreed on things in their relationship, but when it came to raising their children, they were on the same page word for word.

For example, when it came to dealing with school matters, they were both at every Parent-Teacher Conference ready to go over every grade with our teachers. It's kind of hard to mess up in school when your parents go to the meetings, give the teachers their work and home number and tell them to not hesitate to call. They were also prone to pop up visits. I nearly busted a main artery when my dad showed up because my teacher sent a letter home due to my inability to stop talking so much during class. And my mother, as busy as she was, was known by all of our teachers.

When I started Junior High, my mom dropped me off and with the requisite spitting on a tissue to clean my face and a good-bye I thought she was gone. But oh, no she had only gone to park the car. Before I knew it, here comes Ilene. She took my hand and led me inside the school, past the line of parents waiting to speak to settle issues with the administrative office. I said, "Mom all these people are waiting," she replied, "We're just going to say hi to the Principal". So here I am, first day of school and my mom is yelling, "Hi, yoo, hoo, Mr. Brown this is my last one, the baby, Dahlia!" He walked over and shook my hand and then my mom said, "Keep an eye on her, okay?" Let me tell you, my heart skipped a beat, but not in a good way.

Make sure you're on the same page when it comes to raising your children. Parenting is a partnership that should be run like a corporation, which means that all job titles must be filled and no stone left unturned. My parents played every role from head cook to bottle washer. They were the disciplinarians, the breadwinners, the educators, the leaders and on top of it all, they still provided us with lots of love and stability.

# YOU MUST TEK ME FOR A FOOL

I grew up in a household where what my parents said was the law. For example, when it came to watching TV, my parents insured that my sisters and I didn't watch TV all day by being diligent when it came to enforcing their rules. Like most children, we used to watch TV when we weren't supposed to, but somehow my mom always found out. It took us forever to figure out how she knew - she used to feel if the back of the TV was hot. Foiled, we came up with Plan B, which was to turn the TV off during commercials and also fan it so that it would cool down - for future reference that doesn't work.

My mom moved on to her own Plan B - she unplugged the TV. We plugged it back in, but yet again she found out that we watched it. How did she know? How? How?! We had put the TV back on the correct channel and let it cool down. As it turns out, when she unplugged the TV, my mom placed the cord in a certain way so that she could tell if it was moved. Pretty sneaky, sis! And for every infraction where we went against the rules, viewing time was taken away from us.

I mentioned this incident to my mother the other day, to which she responded, "You must've taken me for a fool." My parents were diligent and made sure we abided by their rules.

# WHAT IS A LOVE BOAT?

Remembering the day my mother discovered the TV show 'The Love Boat' still makes me laugh. It was Saturday night and my sisters and I had finished our homework and completed all our chores. Dishes washed? Check! House vacuumed? Check! Everything dusted? Check! Check! Check! So by the rules set forth by my parents, we should have been able to watch TV free and clear. However, we didn't count on one thing - my mother walking through the living room just as the theme of the 'Love Boat' began to play. You remember how it goes, "Love, exciting and new come aboard we're expecting you.... The love boat..." "Love Boat? What is a love boat?" she asked in her thick Jamaican accent. We scrambled to explain that Isaac was the bartender and that although Doc was a ladies man, he was harmless. But based on the theme song, she had already made up her mind that 'The Love Boat' was Babylon on the high seas! My mom promptly sent us to our beds with no TV. 'Fantasy Island', which aired after it, was out as well!

Every generation has levels of inappropriate shows with which to contend. However, no matter what year it is, it is up to parents to monitor what their children are watching. You can't do that if they have a TV, cable or a VCR in their room. The television should be centrally located so you can readily hear and see what's being watched. And it's up to you to turn it off if what's being watched doesn't mesh with your values. The good thing about the whole experience is that my mother took the time to watch the show and enjoyed it quite a bit as I could tell from all the laughter.

The following weekend, she allowed us to watch it. My parents didn't need a rating in the corner of the TV screen to designate parental guidance standards. They just did their jobs. Did it make them popular? No, but they were parents and one of their responsibilities was to keep inappropriate television shows out of our reach.

# A HARD HEAD MAKES
## FOR A SOFT BATTY (BOTTOM)

My parents believed in their children being well behaved, so they had little tolerance for whining. What they said was the law while you were living under their roof. As adults, we can use force, threats or ultimatums to influence people - by the way I am not advocating any of these methods of coercion. The only way children have of exerting their will, is by whining to such a high degree that their parents will eventually give in to get them to stop the racket. Children are egocentric by nature and whining is an egocentric behavior because it puts the whiner's needs above everyone else's. Do like Ilene and Locksley did – don't give in!

Giving in to whining makes children stronger and in effect tells them that whining works. Little whiners that go unchecked turn into big whiners who make everyone else's lives miserable because they don't understand the concept of 'No'. The world is full of people who act out inappropriately when they don't get their way. Jails are full of people who don't understand that they can't have everything they want without regard for laws or the will of others. Now I'm not saying that your child will end up in jail if you let them whine, but you can't deny that a commonality among most people who are incarcerated is that they exerted their will on someone without taking no for an answer. Help your child understand that the sun does not rise and set because they exist.

# YOU'VE GOT A BRAIN RIGHT? USE IT!

My cousin Alan, who is successful today, was getting in legal trouble in his teens. Everyone tried to set him straight, but the truth is that he knew right from wrong. Years later, Alan told me something that my father said that helped him put everything into perspective. My dad got him on the phone and asked, "You've got a brain right?" Alan replied "Yes, Uncle," my dad said, "then use it." Pretty simple, huh?

I'm not saying it's always that simple to get someone to turn his or her life around - and yet sometimes it is. My father didn't give Alan a huge lecture about the perils of his actions. Being a man of few words, my father broke his 'philosophy' down into the simplest terms and the effect was like splashing Alan with a bucket of cold water. In Alan's words he 'woke up' that day. He realized that he could and should be doing better. By asking Alan if he had a brain, my father not only forced him to face his reality, he also forced him to think his actions all the way through to the consequences.

My sisters and I knew the consequences for each of our misdeeds. Most of the time knowing the punishment stopped us from getting into trouble, but being children we sometimes took our chances. A child who is allowed to live 'without using their brain,' will more than likely not make the connection between actions and consequences and will probably get into more than their share of trouble.

# "NO MAN CAN SERVE TWO MASTERS"

*- Matthew: 6:24*

One night, I asked my parents if I could watch TV while I ate dinner. My father replied, "You can't serve two masters at one time." I thought to myself, why is he talking about slavery when all I want to do is watch TV while I eat dinner? I soon came to understand that master meant activities, not actual people. And I'm not talking about multi-tasking. Multi-tasking done properly is great. No, this goes to the heart of getting your child to focus on one thing at a time.

Nowadays, there are tons of people who are trying to serve two, three even ten masters at the same time. I have personally witnessed too many people swerve, nearly run over pedestrians and not obey traffic laws because they haven't mastered how to talk on the phone and operate a two ton vehicle at the same time.

Teach your child from an early age how to focus on one task at a time. Learning how to concentrate is the key. And based on the principles of evolution, we have to ask ourselves if we are sacrificing an important cognitive skill because we allow our children and ourselves to be distracted by TV, computers, phones and all the 'conveniences' of life?

# FIRE DE A MUS MUS TAIL, HIM TINK A COOL BREEZE

*(A rat's tail is on fire and he thinks there's a cool breeze a.k.a. clueless people)*

As a child, I guess you could say I was clueless. That may be harsh, but essentially children are clueless on many levels because of their innocence. I didn't know that I shouldn't be able to do everything I wanted, so my parents set up guidelines to help protect me. When I was in junior high school, my best friend lived up the block. I didn't even have to cross the street to get to her building. Before I went to her apartment, she had to get permission from her parents and I had to get permission from mine. The time I would arrive was confirmed and the time I was to head home was set. When it was time for me to leave, she and her brothers sometimes walked me home, otherwise I would call my parents to say I was heading home and if I wasn't at my doorstep in 120 seconds flat, all hell would break loose.

My parents were very strict when it came to time. In today's world, where it seems like children are getting snatched by total strangers left and right, my parents' strict parenting style would definitely pay off. Their way of life meant treating the word; 'parenting' like a verb - make it an action and be active.

# BREAK THEM EARLY

My father and I have had some of the greatest talks. During one of our pow-wows, we got onto the topic of child rearing and he told me, "Well, you have to break them early." When I told a good friend what he said, her reply was, "Break them early? You mean like horses?" to which I said, "Yeah, well I guess so." I hadn't thought of it that way and though it sounds harsh, there is truth to that statement.

From as early as I can remember, I've always had rules and consequences. We were supposed to get good grades. If we didn't, then we had to study harder and we'd lose TV and play time. I remember my sister Sophia was messing up pretty badly in school. My parents warned her to improve and told her that the consequence would be not being able to go to California for the summer to visit relatives. I hoped my parents wouldn't stick to their word, but summer came and my sister Alecia and I went to California without her.

When they're young, you have to break children of bad behaviors and habits. The best way to do that is with consequences. That way, they have some control over their destiny. To this day, Sophia remembers that lesson and going forward she definitely took my parents' ultimatums more seriously. Just as importantly, I also carry her lesson with me to this day.

## **<u>Chapter Seven</u>**

You Sound Like A Cow
Chewing Its Cud!

# FIX YOUR FACE!

Embarrassing my parents was not really an option because they didn't tolerate bad behavior. I remember being made to go to the birthday party of one of my mother's co-workers. I didn't want to go because I'd have to get dressed up and I wouldn't know anyone. I started to pout, but my mom wasn't having it. She yelled, "Fix your face!" She wasn't talking about putting on make up. She meant to slap on a smile before going out into the world. As a child, it was important for me to learn that I would not always be able to get my way and in those times when I don't; I have to put my best face forward.

They taught me how to slap on a smile and do what's necessary to get through any situation with grace. That's a life lesson that has served me well through the years. Even on my worst days, on most occasions people would not be able to guess what's going on in my world and that's the way it should be.

# BROKE OUT LIKE A SORE FOOT

There are a couple of things I love about the south - warm weather, sweet tea and salutations. I can never get enough of "Yes, ma'am" and "No, ma'am". I love going to the store or a restaurant and being referred to as ma'am. Now I'm not eighty-five, sixty-four or even fifty-five, but my parents taught me to use sir and ma'am or Mr. and Mrs. when addressing adults. Although times have changed, teach your child the formal way of addressing adults so at least they know the difference. Don't let them be the one who is 'broke out like a sore foot.'

In college, while my classmates seemed all too comfortable addressing our professors by their first names, it was hard for me. The best I could do was to refer to my all time favorite teacher Dr. Dwyer as Dr. D. If you want to equip your child with as much knowledge and life skills as possible, then arm them so that they can walk into any situation and at least know how to address people properly.

# WHAT YOU DO AT HOME
# YOU'LL DO IN ROME

Whenever my mom sees someone acting like they have no manners, she loves to say, "Ummm, hmmm, what you do at home, you'll do in Rome." My sister Sophia could pop her bubble gum a mile a minute... that is until my mother caught wind of it and made her stop. And as I write this in a chain coffee store, a guy has his feet up on a table. The same table where people eat and drink. It's taking all of my energy to not walk over and ask him whether he puts his feet up on his dining room table at home...but you know what? I already know the answer. We couldn't put our feet up on furniture at home, so we didn't do it at the dentist's office. We couldn't blow our nose at the dinner table, so we didn't do it while dining with friends.

There were certain behaviors that were labeled inappropriate for public display such as clipping our nails, picking our teeth and flossing. I have had the misfortune to witness all of these behaviors out in public and in the work place. And if we acted like we had no home training, my mom would have the Jamaican equivalent of a kinipschen. Don't let your child be the one who isn't allowed back to a friend's house because they have no manners.

# OUT OF ORDER

In Jamaica, when you say someone is 'out of order,' you're saying that they're rude. The place where my sister Alecia and I got our hair styled when we were younger was part beauty shop and part barbershop. You had to walk through the barbershop to get to the beauty shop. At the age of twelve or thirteen, I was deathly shy. My sister Alecia is also pretty quiet, so when we would enter the hair shop, we would quickly walk to the back and take a seat.

Well, word got back to Ilene that her daughters were not greeting the barbers and other patrons when they walked into the shop. My mom told us that under no circumstances were we to ever enter an establishment and not acknowledge the people inside. We weren't trying to be rude, but our shyness was no excuse for not being polite. So, from that day forward when I enter an establishment, a party or even an elevator, I smile or say hi to the people I encounter. God forbid it got back to Ilene that one of her children was being 'out of order!'

## **Chapter Eight**

# What Sweet Nanny Goat A Go Run Him Belly?

*(Use caution)*

# LATCH KEY KIDS

A child being in an empty home is not the ideal situation, but with the way some families are structured, it is often necessary. If your child is old enough to be home alone, but you still worry about their safety, there are ways to put your mind at ease. When we were old enough to go home alone, my parents laid out some hard and fast rules that we had to abide by in order to be safe.

First of all, we always walked home from school together. When we arrived at our apartment door, we would ring our neighbor's bell. She was expecting us because this had all been pre-arranged. She would stand at her door until we all went inside and locked our door. Once at home, we were not allowed to answer the phone. And this was before call waiting and answering machines, so if my parents called and the line was busy they knew we were on the phone. If they needed us, they would call, let the phone ring once and then call back so we'd know they were on the line.

We were also instructed to never, ever answer the door under any circumstance. And we didn't, so there was never a fear of anyone impersonating an authority figure gaining access to our apartment. Everyone who came to our home made prior arrangements and if they didn't, they found an 'empty' home. I still use that tactic to this day. Even if I am at home listening to music or talking on the phone and the person on the other side of my apartment door can hear me inside, I don't feel any obligation to answer the door.

## TIS HE WHO FIGHT AND RUN AWAY LIVE TO FIGHT ANOTHER DAY

When I was growing up, the bully on my block was a girl named Anissa. Anissa towered over everyone, had a mean scar on the left side of her face and was always looking to start trouble with someone. So, whenever I saw her coming, I would cross the street. On the rare occasion, I would 'buck up pon her' I played it cool. She could verbally assault me all she wanted as long as she didn't put her hands on me. But I was prepared to fight back.

My parents were very clear when it came to fighting. Their edict was don't start fights, EVER. However, if someone hit me, I had permission to defend myself. Don't take away your child's power to defend themselves. Often children don't fight back because they're afraid of getting in trouble with their parents. Share your childhood bully stories, even if you were the bully - there are lessons to be learned from both sides of the fence.

Teach them ways to avoid trouble, like sitting at the front of the school bus by the driver or let them know that sometimes silence is your best weapon. People will say anything to get a rise out of you, so teach your child how to not escalate the situation by getting into a verbal war that might lead to a physical altercation. And when all else fails, sometimes it's best to walk away or even run.

# CROSS ON THE GREEN
# AND NOT IN BETWEEN

As children, before we left our apartment, besides the pre-approval process we had to go through to make sure we could go to a friend's house and the clothes inspection to make sure we weren't running around looking like a bunch of ragamuffins, we had to promise that we would do the following - 'Cross on the Green and Not In Between.' That was a popular slogan and the purpose was to teach children a mantra to help them safely navigate the streets.

There are a lot of things you need to teach your children in order to keep them safe when they are not in your presence because the world is a dangerous place. Is it more dangerous today than when you were growing up? Maybe, so prepare your child for the moment when you're not around and someone wants to harm them. We are always told to respect our elders, to do what an authority figure tells us. As an overall rule that might be right, but give your children permission to trust their instinct and use their sense of fear and intuition to take action.

My parents taught us to never talk to strangers. My mom even went so far as to tell us the following scenario, "Suppose someone pulls up in a car to ask you for directions? By the time you walk over to the car to help them, someone else could come up behind you and push you in the car or the person in the car could grab pull you inside." That was pretty powerful because it didn't leave much to the imagination. And if you think about it, why would a strange adult need a child's help? Having such specific instructions helped keep us safe on Brooklyn's streets. My parents let us know that it's okay to be wrong about a potentially dangerous situation and that it's actually better to be wrong and safe, then right and in harm's way.

# EVERYDAY THE BUCKET A GO A WELL ONE DAY THE BOTTOM A GO DROP OUT

Growing up, I had a best friend and we were inseparable, which works for some people, but after five years I felt as though I no longer had an individual identity. Back in those days, people just automatically assumed we would always be together which is probably what makes two people 'best' friends. But finally, it got to the point where I wrongly resented my friend because I felt like I was suffocating.

At the age of fourteen, I didn't have the skills to communicate needing space so instead I found ways to always be 'busy'. In hindsight, it would have been great if I could have found a way to have my friendship and still be able to have a separate circle of friends, rather than making the choice between the two. But hanging out all day, every day, turned out to be an overload and eventually the bottom surely dropped out of that 'bucket.'

Teach your child the importance of doing things in moderation because overuse only diminishes the shelf life of whatever is the object of constant wear and tear.

# MEK SURE YOU'RE INA YARD
# WHEN DE SUN GUH DOWN

One of the many rules that my mother had to follow when she was growing up was that she and her siblings had to be at home – 'ina yard' – when the sun went down. That way they wouldn't become prey to the pitfalls that often come with adolescence. As a matter of fact, she could only remember one time when she and two of her brothers were allowed to go to a big party in the district. They were allowed to go, but with a very stern warning from my grandfather, "Anyhow, trouble find its way to the party you mek sure you find your way home!"

Sure enough, a fight broke out and rather than heading home, my mother and uncles took the chance that my grandfather wouldn't find out. St. Elizabeth may be the second largest parish in Jamaica, but news traveled fast, especially when you consider the fact that to this day my grandparents don't have a phone. So here comes my grandfather all six foot, five inches of him. Knowing that nothing short of Jesus Christ walking on water again could save them, my mom and her brothers jumped over fences and scrambled through brush to hightail it home, so that they wouldn't get caught. When my grandfather said something, he meant it and he had a very 'hands on' approach to childrearing.

As underage children, my sisters and I weren't allowed to attend parties if my parents didn't know the adults responsible for the function. If they couldn't talk to the person in charge, then the answer to, "Can I go to the party?" was no. We definitely knew not to ask if we couldn't provide a phone number and physical address. These few measures decreased our chances of falling into pitfalls. And just like my mother, we were instructed to leave should there be trouble.

These rules may not make your child the most popular person in school, but they won't be unduly exposed to harm either. My parents also exhibited no shame when it came to showing up unexpectedly. Catching children off guard is a great way to instill a healthy dose of fear in them. Fear that if they don't do what's right, they will be caught and incur consequences for their actions.

# SIMMER DOWN

There was no back talking in our home. Even getting angry was out of the question. Anger is a healthy emotion, so give your children permission to be angry as long as it's in a non-destructive manner. I grew up in a household where children were to be seen and not heard, so all through my early adulthood I had trouble expressing anger. When I was young, I would hold in my anger. As an adult, I used to contain my anger, but walked around seething, looking for a reason to explode.

Now, I meditate, exercise, do yoga and when someone cuts me off in traffic, rather then letting road rage get the best of me, I flash the peace sign 95% of the time. It throws people off and makes them realize how silly it is to play cat and mouse with a total stranger.

# SPLIFFS AND TINGS

In 1982, my parents threw my sister Sophia a Sweet Sixteen party in our apartment. We went out and bought a lot of the hottest rap and R&B records. My parents moved all of the furniture out of their bedroom so there was a dance floor, and a couple of aunts and uncles came over to hang with my parents. I fell asleep early, but not before someone decided to light up a spliff – a joint. I guess the perpetrator assumed that all Jamaicans smoked dope. Well, they were wrong because as soon as the scent reached my parents, all you heard was the needle go *riiiiiip!* as it was dragged off the record. The lights went on full blast and my dad stood in the middle of the room; giving all in attendance a look that could have melted a glacier. I'm sure he only looked around for about sixty seconds, but it felt like sixty years. He didn't say a word; he just gave the old evil eye, turned around, left the room and never had to return,

There can't be any ambiguity about your stance on substance abuse because where curiosity and confusion meet, curiosity will almost always win with a child. Be ready for the talk about substance abuse with your children. Also be age appropriate when it comes to revealing your past. Does your twelve-year-old really need to know that you drank your first beer at their age? The last thing you want is your past being used as an excuse by your child for bad behavior.

# IF A FISH COULD KEEP HIM MOUTH
# SHUT HIM NEVER WOULD GET CAUGHT

I was in junior high school when I learned a very important life lesson about staying out of other people's disagreements. Yes, sometimes intervention is needed, but unless it's an emergency it probably is best to let people fight their own battles. Two friends were having a disagreement and some people, like me chose sides, while others remained neutral. I supported one friend in the argument while shunning the other. However, when the two of them reconciled, I was left 'holding the bag' so to speak because I never had a reason to get involved in the first place.

Life is complicated enough without throwing in the problems of others. Let your child know that choosing sides in an argument that does not involve them, whether in business or the playground, is usually a big mistake. The best advice you can give your child in those situations, especially when people may be pressuring them to choose a side is to say, "I don't believe in choosing sides. You're both my friends and so I'm not going to choose," or "I'm sure you can work it out without my involvement."

## Chapter Nine

A New Broom Sweeps Clean,
But An Old Broom
Knows Every Corner

# PRECIOUS AND DEAR

I woke up one morning in Jamaica, to find my grandfather gone and my grandmother beside herself with worry. My grandfather had ridden his bike from Hodgesland, where they live, to Middle Quarters where my Uncle lives, to pick up some mint leaves for tea. When he returned, he was drenched in sweat and pushing his bike up the driveway. My grandmother, who was about to fall over because she had worked herself up into such a tizzy asked, "What took you so long? Me ah sit here ah worry myself to death." Exhausted and still catching his breath, my grandpa replied, "You tink me a cyar (car)? I am not a cyar. I am an old man." I had to laugh at that one. At the age of eighty-three, grandpa was in great shape. He rode his bike several miles down a steep hill and back, without having a heart attack that's pretty impressive.

My grandmother used to treat even the simplest things as if they were worth their weight in gold. She would fold up a paper towel like it was fine silk and then tell me that with the price of things, the paper towel was precious and dear. That term can be applied to many things in life and in particular, to our health. Once you lose your health, there often isn't much you can do to get it back, so treat it like it's precious and dear.

Since I was raised by Jamaicans, I was encouraged to walk as much as possible, play outside and read to keep my mind sharp. Nowadays, grandpa uses a cane or his 'walking stick' to get around when he leaves the house, but other than that he walks on his own. And after nine decades he can cook, clean and groom himself. His way of life now is by design, not by accident.

# MIND YOUR SISTERS

Whatever my older sisters did, I wasn't far behind. They couldn't leave the house without me trailing behind them, but they didn't mind. I can't imagine being an only child. Though I'm sure it has its good points, but in my opinion, nothing beats having siblings. My parents used to tell us often that we must look out for each other and are never to leave anyone behind - by the way, that goes for friends too. My parents always told us that if three of us leave the home, then three of us better come back. Trust me when I say, that wasn't just a suggestion.

Older siblings set the bar for the younger ones, whether they want to or not. So make sure that your eldest is up to the task and let them know they have a responsibility to carry themselves in a way that their younger brothers and sisters can follow. And let your younger children know that they have to 'mind' what their older siblings say and they should have each other's backs.

# 'NUFF LOVE

When I messed up in school, my dad would sit me down and give me the 'Immigrant Speech.' I'll paraphrase, "You know, your mother and I came to this country to give unu a better life. Life, it hard in Jamaica, life in America easy. To get to school, you have a school bus fi pick you up. You know what I had fi do to get to school? Me have fi walk tree hundred miles each way ina snow!" (The latter part of his story is known as skylarking since there's no snow in Jamaica). My dad also told me that as the only Yankee in the family, I could be the president of the United States if I wanted.

No one is an angel, so my parent's love was not a condition of good behavior - they loved me regardless of whether I talked too much in class, which was very often, received a bad grade on a test or broke the vacuum cleaner. Speaking from a child's perspective, I can confidently say that there's something very comforting about a parent's love. There's nothing like it in the world – your siblings, your friends or even your mate can't give it to you. My parents gave me 'nuff love and in return got 'nuff respect.

## Chapter Ten

If You're Born to Hang,
You Cyan't Drown

# WHEN TROUBLE HIT
# PICKNEY SHIRT FITS!

A man in New York City jumped into the path of an oncoming subway train to save a total stranger. My mom and I were discussing his heroism when she commented, "When trouble hit pickney (a child's) shirt fits." What she was trying to convey was that when painted into a corner, some people will go above and beyond what the average person would do, in the same situation.

A true testament of a person's values is how they act when they are caught off guard. Do you know how your child would act if a friend was drowning? There are no guarantees, but give your child specific instruction regarding what is and is not acceptable behavior. A good example of that is when my parents taught us to always look out for each other.

One day after school, I was waiting for my sisters so that we could walk home together, when a boy started physically pushing me around. I told him to leave me alone, but he wouldn't. I didn't know what to do, but luckily my sister Sophia did. She showed up on the scene; wielding her heavy wooden clogs like a pair of nunchucks – I did mention we were raised Jamaican, right? That bully never bothered me again. And she didn't get in trouble with my parents because she was doing as she was taught, which was to defend her baby sister.

# A COW NEVER KNOWS THE USE
# OF ITS TAIL UNTIL IT'S GONE

As a child, when I discovered the concept of death, I became very afraid of dying. So, I came up with a system of how I thought everyone in the world should die. I thought it only fair that we should die alphabetically, by last name. Using that theory, it would take death quite some time to get around to me all the way back in the W's.

I don't know if it's luck or just because my family seems to live forever, but I have only had four major deaths in my life - my paternal grandfather and grandmother, an uncle who I absolutely adore to this day and an aunt who meant the world to me. Before both my aunt and uncle succumbed to cancer, they told me something that is very comforting. In their own way, they both said, "What people don't realize is that when it's your time to go, you're ready," knowing that brings me a measure of peace.

My mom constantly tells my sisters and I, "Don't wait until I'm gone to buy me flowers." That is a very true statement and also a plug on her part to get more flowers. How many family members or friends are you not talking to because of disagreements? Show your children through your actions that you value life. Loving yourself and those around you is the best way to do that.

# NIGH NIGHT OR SET OUT

In 1998, when my maternal grandmother turned ninety, we went down to Jamaica and gave her a big party. We spread the word through the district and cooked tons of food. The party was so huge that a vendor set up a jerk stand at the end of the driveway and another vendor walked through the crowd selling cashews and peanuts. It was a lot of fun. Sitting with my grandmother on the veranda, I marveled at the number of people in attendance. I said to her, "Wow, grandma look at all the people who showed up to help you celebrate your birthday." She replied, "Hmph, dem no come fi see me, dem only come for de food!" We had a good laugh.

In 1999, almost a year to the day, my grandmother passed away, we were back in Jamaica to send her home; the number of people who showed up for her Nigh Night or Set Out, which is a party celebrating one's passing, was just as huge. I remember my uncles grabbing pots and pans to drum on and a DJ set up a sound system so that people could sing and dance through the night. My grandmother's passing was the first death of a close family member that I ever experienced.

It was a great lesson because it showed me that when someone goes 'home,' rather than sitting around being depressed, we should celebrate their life and I mean really celebrate. And I think the Nigh Night also helped take the edge off my grandmother's passing for even my young family members, because it showed that death doesn't have to be an entirely scary thing. That time in Jamaica is actually one of my favorites because we shared stories about grandma, which brought us closer as a family. Even my grandfather, who normally didn't talk about the past, opened up about his life with grandma.

By celebrating and talking about our loved ones, we show that the dearly departed may be gone physically, but never forgotten. And that their passing is nothing to be sad about. That night, as everyone drank and partied in Ms. Ella's honor, once again we were out on the veranda when I said, "Wow, look at all these people who came to see grandma go home!" My mom and sisters said in unison, "Hmph dem no come fi see her, dem only come for de food!"

## **Chapter Eleven**

# What Is For You
# Can't Be Un-For You

# EVERY DOG HAS ITS DAY
# AND EVERY PUSS
# HAS ITS TWELVE O'CLOCK

I was in high school when my parents separated. At the time, I felt so lost it was like my whole world was crashing around me. I tried to distract myself by getting into activities at school. I was an okay swimmer, but thought if I could just make the team; at least things would start looking up. I tried out and didn't make the squad. That compounded with the turmoil at home was devastating. I was probably sixteen or seventeen at the time and I thought my world was over. But guess what? I'm still here. Life goes on and I've had a lot more good times than bad. The times when I got the job or received the writing award meant that someone else didn't and vice versa.

From day to day, sometimes our best will not be good enough to get the job or the last spot on the team or even win the heart of that special boy or girl. No one knows how long his or her time to shine will last. Andy Warhol speculated that we get fifteen minutes, but some people get a day or a year, while others get only a couple of hours. It's not the length of time you get to be on top, it's what you do while you're there. Today may be someone else's day, but eventually you will get your twelve o'clock.

# THE HIGHER THE MONKEY CLIMB
# THE MORE HIM EXPOSE

When you're young, it's hard to not want to be a part of the 'in' crowd. I started high school in my sophomore year, rather than as a freshman like everyone else, so my classmates had a leg up on me when it came to making friends and being part of a click. I was so painfully shy and unpopular that I joined the computer squad just to avoid eating lunch by myself.

In every setting, there will always be the popular people and I have to admit that I wanted to be one of them, until I realized how much of a target they were. Yes, people wanted to be around them and hang out with them, but they were also under constant attack regarding their integrity, sexual prowess, appearance, everything.

Knowing what I know now, I don't let the fear of being judged by others hold me back from excelling, but I definitely move through life with an awareness of how the higher you go in life or your career the more you are open to criticism.

## **Chapter Twelve**

Ray, Ray, Ray

*(etc., etc., etc.)*

# EAT AIR PIE AND NOTHING CHOPS

Back in her day, my mother's idea of a treat was to chase the molasses truck with her cohorts, so that they could lick the sweet molasses off the back of the truck. What I would have paid to have that truck slam on its breaks... but I digress. Children will eat you out of house and home, according to my mother, if you let them. My parents taught us how not to be glutinous by not indulging our every food whim. They didn't starve us, but if they bought snacks and we ate them all in one day, oh well, the next time we were hungry we had to eat air pie and nothing chops. Truth be told, children will find snacks if they can't wait until mealtime. My personal favorite was syrup on Wonder bread. And by monitoring our eating habits, they taught us to eat in moderation, which has translated to a healthy diet for life.

# COME BACK TO JAMAICA, WHAT'S OLD IS WHAT'S NEW

On my last trip back to Jamaica, I went solo, which is actually a pretty big deal because my grandfather lives in the country and it's missing a lot of the comforts of home, i.e. Internet access, more than two TV stations and indoor plumbing with strong water pressure. My grandfather has two water tanks, but when I was there it hadn't rained for a while; so the one used for showers and the kitchen had run dry. I needed water to bathe and wash dishes, so I had to use the one at the foot of the house. The one, which to paraphrase my mom, "I was de only gyal and me haffi help build de tank ina dress. Me haffi carry rock stone up and down de hill with me bare hands dem!" - cue the violins.

So, the process is you have to bail water with a small bucket from the tank, into a larger bucket that you carry up to the house. Sound like 'Survivor?' No, that's my Jamaican 'vacation.' I am not tall enough to throw the bucket into the tank, so under the watchful eye of my ninety one-year-old grandfather I climbed on top of it, so that I could use my body weight to bail the water. All the while grandpa is calling out from the veranda, "Mind you nuh fall in! Mind you nuh fall in! Me cyan't come get you! Me cyan't come get you! Lawd Jesus de pickney going fi fall in!"

I reassure grandpa that I will not fall into the tank. I bail the water and as I'm pouring it into the bigger bucket water splashes all over the place. Grandpa calls out, "Look how de pickney a splash de water all over de place!" I call back, "I'll be more careful grandpa," all the while I'm thinking to myself this was not in the Air Jamaica brochure!!! The big bucket is full and so now comes the task of carrying the bucket up the rocky walkway to the kitchen. I guess it'd be too much to ask that the ground be paved.

As I'm walking or should I say struggling to make my way to the kitchen, here's grandpa again with his running commentary, "What a way she ah splash de wata outa de bucket. You nah have any left by de time you reach de kitchen!" I reply, "Don't worry grandpa; there will be plenty of water left when I get to the house." I say this right before I almost bust my backside because the ground and my flip-flops are sopping wet. I somehow make it to the kitchen in one piece, pour out the water and head back down to the tank to bail water another three or four times.

I often dreamt about building my grandparents a big house with a washer and dryer, so when I visit I don't have to use a washboard and clothesline to clean and dry my clothes. I would somehow get this new home wired with electricity that didn't go out every time there's a storm. And of course there would have to be a phone, so that I wouldn't have to go to Black River to buy a phone card and then borrow a cell phone to make calls. And it goes without saying, there'd be no outhouse.

Yes, I used to dream about all the modern conveniences that I would provide my grandparents, but would they truly be better off? What is so great about having 500 cable channels, text messages every two seconds and an indoor bathroom – okay, forget the last part but you know what I mean. Because we don't have a million and one distractions, when I go back to Jamaica my grandfather and I spend time talking; he tells me about how he came to America in WWII as a migrant worker and we play dominoes all day, every day except Sunday because, "The Lawd said we fi rest pon Sunday."

We sit out on the veranda at night and while the mosquitoes are having a field day with my fresh American blood, grandpa barely twitches. And I get to do something I rarely do here in America, I get to look up and see a sky filled with stars every night.

So for me at least, going back to Jamaica combines what's old with what's new, because I learn a lot about my family and history but I learn so much more about myself.

# WALK GOOD!

'Walk Good' is a goodbye wish that you say when you part company. It's a way of saying to someone that they should make their way through their day/life safely and the 'right' way. I often gripe about how bad I had it, growing up. Especially when you look around at children today who are getting all their whims satisfied at the drop of a hat. Navigating life can be hard at times, but it's a little easier if you receive a road map early in life because even if you stumble and fall, hopefully you'll be able to get back on track. I am lucky because I have parents who took their responsibilities very seriously and never veered off course. They were tough as nails and still are, but I don't begrudge them anything they did while raising me because I'm pretty happy with the way I turned out. Hopefully, you learned something new, had a laugh and will now raise your children like Jamaicans.

*Walk Good Nuh Mon!*

Printed in the United States
103312LV00006B/338/A

9 780615 147611